WHAT WILL LAST

New and Collected Poems

Gus Speth

SHIRES●PRESS

4869 Main Street
P.O. Box 2200
Manchester Center, VT 05255
www.northshire.com

What Will Last
New and Collected Poems
©2021 Gus Speth

ISBN: 978-1-60571-601-5

Cover art, *Michael's Window*, by Gus Speth
Design/production, Anne Pace

Printed in the United States
October 2021

Also by Gus Speth

*Red Sky at Morning: America and the Crisis of the
Global Environment*

*The Bridge at the Edge of the World: Capitalism, the
Environment, and Crossing from Crisis to Sustainability*

America the Possible: Manifesto for a New Economy

Angels by the River: A Memoir

What We Have Instead: Poems

It's Already Tomorrow: Poems

The New Systems Reader: Alternatives to a Failed Economy

*They Knew: The US Federal Government's Fifty-Year Role
in Causing the Climate Crisis*

WHAT WILL LAST

New and Collected Poems

Gus Speth

For Catherine, Jim, and Charlie

— CONTENTS —

1

Hope and Beyond

2

People and Places

CONTENTS

3

Save Time To Smile

Author's Note

What reality was ever created by realists?
…What we cannot dream we can never do.

Richard Flanagan

1

Hope and Beyond

Independence Day

If I could be what I'm clearly not,
I would lay my hands upon the world,
call down a blessing of peace and freedom
from hunger, pain, illiteracy and oppression.
I would appoint an ambassador
to every living species and grant them
plenipotentiary powers of protection,
just as I would grant such powers to all
mothers for their children and charges.
I would bring hosannas to Pope Francis,
Thomas Berry and Reverend Barber,
and to 21 kids who sued for climate
against government by failure.
I would call upon the Devil,
for who would know better,
to disclose every rancid scheme
and deplorable machination
of the rich and powerful, including
those hiding under corporate shells.
I would pardon all those unjustly
imprisoned or prosecuted. And
I would forgive all those gullible
and duped or simply uninformed,
not requiring their repentance but
merely a promise to use good sense—
while we all remember the truth
self-evident at the Founding
that we are all created equal.

It's Time for America Again

I think I see America again.
Every time she seems so lost,
America finds a touch of sane.

Social injustice is a dark stain.
But in countless civil protests,
I think I see America again.

Democracy's hard to sustain.
Before democracy is lost,
America finds a bit of sane.

Polluters have had free rein.
Now there may be climate action.
I think I see America again.

Migrant treatment's not humane.
Decency demands a better tack.
Will America find a touch of sane?

Time now for a bold campaign:
a struggle for all the children.
It's time for America again.

Random Sample

I am not a robot
lots of online chatter
everybody knows
into a ton of trouble
try this new paella
running out of time
who was in charge
pre-K subcommittee deadlocked
something never seen before
a disastrophy, the young girl said
what will happen next
anti-semitic material found
moose population down, ticks blamed
I'm tired, so very tired
second Capitol attack
sign my name and say good-bye
your Dropbox is full
where can I sit down
FBI says tips are up
herbal immune support is here
your cup needs some sweet
pain always leaves a gift
honey, we're the big door prize
squeeze me, I squeak

Falling Apart

It was a fall to remember
It left a big hole in my heart
Foliage was never prettier
In the fall of falling apart

He left a big hole in my heart
A dog that was easy to love
In the fall of falling apart
We went together hand in glove

A dog that was easy to love
Smart and he could be ornery
We went together hand in glove
He had many ways to tease me

Smart and he could be ornery
He knew his words and tried to talk
He had many ways to tease me
Gave me a grin when he balked

He knew his words and tried to talk
He leaves a big hole in my heart
Stayed close when we went for a walk
In the fall of falling apart

Dogs find us to teach us about love
And leave us to teach about loss
It is a love we hope to be worthy of
But one that comes with a cost

A Place Beyond

Beyond all our fears, it is.
Beyond grieving and crying, it is.
Beyond even hope, it is.
What then is left beyond?

A collapse of sentiment?
What do they feel:
the Black man in solitary,
the young girl buried
in the rubble of Aleppo,
the Amazon biologist
watching the forest die?

What do we feel, you and I?
Can the mere knowledge
of the world's desperation
while still in a sheltered space
take us to a place beyond?

I can only speak for myself.
I hunger to strike a blow
so shattering that enthrallment
breaks into a million shards
and falls to the feet of the world.

Killing Time

Where is today today?
It is so easy to miss.
It comes on quiet puppy feet
bringing juicy burgers and
good ideas for killing time.
Then it stealthily slips away,
and we sink into the morrow.

What He Could Have Done

He could have pitched a tent in Lafayette Square
and stopped eating until real action on climate change.
He thought about it many times, imagined reporters
seeking his views as he sat outside his little tent.

Yet even his fantasy slipped to the
possibility of fasting away instead in a
Hay-Adams room overlooking the park.
No reason not to be comfortable, and besides
he would get more reporters that way.
Along with water, he thought,
should I take a vitamin every day?

Amid the great suffering of the world,
he had lived a life of worldly comfort.
He did a bit of time in jail for protesting
the end of the world as we know it.

Not risking everything is a strategy
that ends with grandkids deprived.
He knows that now, deeply knows
this is no time for self-deception.
But will he act on his conviction?

Holding It All Together

I can't imagine
the world working
when I'm gone
or if I just quit.

The guidance I give
shouting at the TV,
cursing in the yard,
advising friends what to think,
giving assignments to reporters,
holds the world together,
such as it is.

Coping is what it's all about.
Pissing in the wind,
whistling past the graveyard,
these are life skills
learned in lesser times
and now invoked.

As the proper order of the world
seems rather threatened,
and the supplies of comity,
discretion, and common decency run short,
still, we will confound the world
with civility and thoughtful observation
while going berserk at home
where oaths echo
from wall to wall.

Making Music

He had no music left in him.
It was there once, upon a time.
He was young then and strong,
a bubbling cauldron of words
and tunes to go along.

But the blows came quickly.
Deep drink, it helped to dampen
what the Stan war did to his boy.
Then his lady gone with cancer.
Nothing of joy left to destroy.

He was unmoored, adrift.
He knew he had to move on.
Travel America with his dog?
Head for an island somewhere?
Just make that past to fade to fog.

He wanted mainly to escape.
A friend said "find a moose."
He looked at wildlife maps,
and headed for northeast Vermont,
a hotspot for moose mishaps.

He found an old ramshackle farm
perched up the flank of Burke Mountain.
Worked a bit at the ski resort.
Did odd jobs for newcomers.
Walked with his bloodhound Snort.

Peace came to visit one spring
as he looked out from his porch
over bogs and fens to the far blue hills.
He put on the first of his old cds,
felt a rush of forgotten thrills.

Townes van Zandt suited his mood;
John Prine was just too damn happy.
But that was changing, he could tell.
He stared at the black guitar case,
still scared to come out of the shell.

But then one day it opened up.
He hit a few chords on the porch.
In Guy Clark's past great song,
it's the guitar that plays the man.
For him, well, that was just plain wrong.

Composing was painfully hard,
so slow he'd forget where he was.
He had no idea what to say.
Passing songbirds distracted him.
Had talent also flown away?

A new girlfriend pointed the way.
"You need to write from life
and not just from memory.
Get rolling man!" she shouted,
"Other people hold the key."

He took a job performing each
evening at a spot down in the town.
He didn't want to be discovered;
that had happened long ago.
But pieces of him had now recovered.

He was never to regain his fame.
A few new songs were recorded.
But he became beloved in town.
He and Jill were soon married,
happy with the life they'd found.

Rodney Crowell's song "It Ain't Over Yet"
became his personal anthem.
And what would bring his friends new highs?
He and Jill singing Prine and Iris DeMent's
"Honey, we're the big door prize."

Listening

It's a stirring sound.
Not Bach in B-minor but
hot coffee nearby.

Listen carefully—
the new puppy is afoot.
Hear today's mischief.

DeMent is singing.
Much-loved songs for the Delta.
It's not far away.

I hear wind outside—
opera of the forest.
That is music too.

Selectively deaf:
tuning out the needless noise.
But I do hear you.

She's giving advice.
I am working on listening.
Unhappy with me.

Let's go to the game!
Gallaudet's winning season.
They're a spunky team.

Clap the big bass drum:
signal to snap the football
where there is no sound.

Hands and fingers shake—
the applause for the touchdown.
Silent. Beautiful.

Which sense to give up?
Some say it should be hearing.
What would students say?

Each sense is precious.
Sight, hearing, smell, taste, feeling.
I must have music.

The Prediction

1.

Early Pandemic, March 2020

A happening across America.
Maybe it sounds early,
just March after all, but
Christmas presents are
being prepared in millions of
homes and apartments,
trailer parks, co-ops and condos.
The project is taken up
watching boring TV shows
or in any vacant room
where the kids won't see.
Some are preparing them
after long delays and neglect.
Others just fell into it naturally
without much thought.
Like a big beautiful quilt,
these presents can't be rushed.
When delivered for Christmas,
there will be joy in the house.

2.

As Things Worked Out, March 2021

So much for prediction!
Pandemic baby boom—a bust.
2020 not generally inviting
to lighthearted pleasures
or dreams, or plans for the future
or lovemaking actually.
A death-filled, pain-filled year
full of stress and fear
anger and frustration—
life as broken fragments
and recycling worries.

A year of loss when
women suffered most deeply:
as the months crept by
jobs lost in record numbers
lost income and security
lost family support and daycare
lost schools, churches, parks
lost freedom, hugging, laughing
lost each other,
and by the end of the day
bone tired, exhausted.

Mother Emanuel

No first stone is cast,
and if no first, none.

So many wrongs.
Our world we'll fill
with forgiveness.

(but)
Remember, forgiveness
does not imply blameless.
It's just the opposite.

(and)
Understanding does not
imply acceptance.
It implies awareness.

(for)
We are all fallen.
Omissions, commissions,
can we forgive ourselves?

(and yet)
Can we also be accountable
for our acts and expect
accountability for others?

Forgiveness can be real,
accountability too.
But forgiveness sometimes exists
on a different plane altogether.

On the 17th of June 2015 Dylann Roof entered Emanuel
AME church in Charleston and shot to death nine
Black church members there for Bible study. A short
while later the families of the victims faced Roof.
"One by one, those who chose to speak at a bond
hearing did not turn to anger. Instead … they offered
him forgiveness and said they were praying for his soul,
even as they described the pain of their losses."
Later, they would oppose putting him to death,
though not putting him in prison.

Visiting Emanuel AME the year after Roof
an elderly Black woman there spoke kindly with me
at length, like I was the one needing comfort.

Forgiveness

I have some vivid memories
I wish were not there

We heard it all the time
in the South in the '50s
That's mighty white of you!
racist words spoken then
as just a casual thank you

I went recently to the
Blacksonian on the Mall
and I left there uplifted
but with moist eyes and cheeks
When I got home I listened
to King speak in Memphis
"I've been to the mountain top"

Gnawing away inside me are
the shootings at Mother Emanuel
the many times Black lives haven't mattered
the mass incarceration
the famine of equal opportunity
the ongoing everyday prejudice

I want to go in supplication
to the Calhoun Street sidewalk
to the Edmund Pettus bridge
to Montgomery's memorial
to four thousand lynchings
and ask there for a forgiveness
that in acts of amazing grace has
already been given so many times

In the End We Make Our Peace

In 1948 the big planes roared
day and night into Berlin's Tegel,
making noises common to large airports.
Yet even those right under the flight path
did not hear noise. Instead they heard:
We are free. We are still free.
The Berlin airlift saved most of the city.

Sometimes I cry for my country.
Whence all the violence and destruction?
We are missing, losing, hurting so.
At times I've almost given up on her.
But I have cried for decades and
I am still flying Old Glory after all.
Much here makes me damn proud.

My wife and I were buddies in pre-school
and married now for fifty-six years.
Too often I know I disappointed her.
Hell, I often disappointed myself.
Stubborn, self-absorbed, inattentive.
It is the great compliment of my life:
despite it all, she keeps me around.

So, we know the bitter and the sweet,
and, in the end, we make our peace.
We hope sweet will outweigh,
and take us to another day.

In the Maritimes

Road sign warns
"Blind Crest" ahead.
Over the hill,
well, anything.
Life unfolds
like hills, blind
to what's ahead.
Then, the crest,
the new horizon.
Perhaps a nice view
Fundy and beyond.
Perhaps sideswiped,
someone texting
his mistress
at the motel.

Life's hills, the daily struggle:
work, meals, schools, doctors,
there is so very much to juggle.
We hope for appreciation,
helps make it worth the trouble.
But we act from our affection—
let some worry with that puzzle.

When life seems one hill on another,
know that your caring is worthy bother.
You have no idea who will come to stand your side.
But when it's done, your peace is that you tried.

The Last Monarch

The season of beautiful endings,
life giving up another round.
At first it seemed heart rending.
The fields turned a rusty brown.

Life giving up another round,
the monarch drifted to the grass.
The fields turned a rusty brown.
Fall has now yes come to pass.

The monarch drifted to the grass,
the maples glowed bright red.
Fall has now yes come to pass,
nature putting herself to bed.

The maples glowed bright red.
Dying away precedes new birth,
nature putting herself to bed.
My footprint too upon this earth.

Dying away precedes new birth,
at first it seemed heart rending.
My footprint too upon this earth.
This season of beautiful endings.

Tomorrow Is a Yesterday Place

Tomorrow, and tomorrow, and tomorrow,
Creeps in this petty pace from day to day,
To the last syllable of recorded time.

Time paused, took in the current scene,
and went away.
The last syllable happened yesterday.
Lord knows exactly what time saw,
but enough to make time withdraw.

So tomorrow is a yesterday place,
a land of many dreams and hope
where today had little space,
a land where even I could cope.

Without tomorrow we must face
the brutal truth of everyday—
the desperations we can't erase,
a place well in old history's sway.

I will cling then to tomorrow!
I will hope it will come back.
With it, there's relief to sorrow,
and a way to get life on track.

2

People and Places

Sarah's Farewell

Now comes New Winter's Day
the shortest of the year
Not much time to say
goodbye to those held dear

The path to Sarah's house
is filled now with snow
A good one to bitch and grouse
she said it's time for me to go

And so she just stopped eating
and convened a celebration
She stood at the door a-greeting
the whole damn congregation

All her friends came that day
Their feelings were complex
Some felt nothing but dismay
Some danced the ice-cold deck

Calmly and peacefully one day
with people who loved her dearly
she silently slipped away her way
Sarah knew her mind so clearly

It is easy to miss someone
who loved my cooking so
On this day of little sun
I feel an afterglow

We thought she was full gone
but I found a message in her desk
"Miss me but do not mourn
I lived well and better than the rest"

Ode to the Tar Snakes Painter

The truck slows down.
He hops off the back,
magic wand in his hand,
the road begs for black.

They try to define who
is an essential worker.
So easily they might miss
the tar snakes painter.

He first must play a bit.
He squirts a Jackson Pollock
and signs in secret script.
Draws rapids he has shot.

Dissolving into fragments,
the road can't bear the freight.
Cracks here and fissures,
he hopes it's not too late.

He paints in vacant spaces,
hot tar seeps and seeks to hold.
It fills and does the binding.
The painter heals the road.

(Who among us knows
what this artist knows
of what the day requires,
where the real work goes?
Work that has benefit,
work that lasts a while,
work that can be fun,
and brings a little smile.
I look at all I've done
and wonder what will last.
Long as a mended road,
or lost back in the past?)

A Place of Little Pretense

This small beach house was built in 1951,
just across the dunes from the big breakers.
Facing the full Atlantic through a few palmettos,
it has survived the ferocity of many encounters,
including the direct hit of the big storm Hugo.
It has survived thousands of children
tracking in tons of sand in wet bathing suits.
It has been the enduring strong cauldron
for explosions of laughter and love and anger.
Its tiny kitchen has seen the endless shucking
of local oysters and the frying of many flounder.

How many books have been read here?
How much coffee spilled into the rugs?
How many exhibitions of grandkids' art?
How many hugs?
How many castles washed away by the waves?
How many games of Monopoly and cards?
How many kids bodysurfed to dad's legs?
How many carbs?
How many shark teeth found near the surf?
How many dogs slept in the chairs?
How many bare feet warmed by the sand?
How many beers?

The signs of age are all around:
tiny worn sinks in upstairs bedrooms,
a bottom floor flat on the ground,
a very small toilet in the bathroom,
the walls and ceiling a simple bare pine,
the medicine cabinet with its slit in the back,
the razor blades there to oblivion assigned.
There is mold around the edges and corners,
lots of rust from sitting in the salty air,
and boards worn out around the dormers.

This house is a modest place on the beach,
yet pilgrims trek here each summer.
It's a state of mind they hope to reach,
to see again their families and each other,
to watch birds and catch some fish,
to worship the tanning sun,
and the boys look at girls, and wish.

Out of Place

Seen from the deck of this
place of little pretense,
the Atlantic today lies flat and leaden,
shrouded in low, lifeless clouds.
I look out from a beachfront bungalow
built in 1951 when I was nine.
It is out of place now,
and we are its final renters.
It cannot match its neighbors,
the cementitious mega-mansions
that up the strand and down
bestride the narrow dunes
crushing the sand crabs
and the small pleasures of everyday life
at a beach once arrogantly shabby.
There are now swimming pools
to my left and also to my right.
Is it just my age pining for the times
we brought our children to this place
and ran along the warm sand path
through the dunes to the beach?
Folly our dog is scared. And why not?
She sees the empty rooms,
furniture gone to Goodwill,
everything we own boxed and bagged
and ready to move on
before the wrecking ball.
It is coming tomorrow.
I am going peacefully,
but I am scared too.

A Gentleman I Knew

Dangling emotions, residue of dreams,
orphaned feeling now attached to nothing.
They linger longer as the years pile up,
while memories rush about, fresh as life.

A cozy room in a large white house.
Mr. Jim in his always chair by the fire.
A chilly Sunday afternoon.
His poker shifts glowing embers of coal.

He is quizzing me in a teasing way.
I struggle to answer why Truman fired MacArthur
while also thinking about "High Noon."
Mr. Jim looks like an older Gary Cooper.

I was told I'd be good company for him.
I make an effort to visit most Sundays.
In his mid 70s, his beloved Claire ill.
It is the year 1958, and I am in high school.

In truth I'm there for his kindness, his interest in me,
his great knowledge. I am lapping it up.
He made up for college reading the Harvard Classics,
fine pencil notes on every page. I looked.

We talk politics. He had despised Joe McCarthy.
He likes Ike, though a life-long Democrat.
He grew up in the mean years after Reconstruction,
but racial hatred is totally alien to him.

As gentle with himself as with others,
he takes out four cigarettes late each day.
Sano brand, they of the powerful filters.
He smokes them over the next hour, and that's it.

Once I used the cigarette lighter in his nice car
to burn little circles in the leather seats.
Now we are close, enjoying each other.
I can tell he is growing me. I like it.

⁓

Mr. Jim is a proper dresser—very proper.
Most often he can be found in a three-piece suit,
a dark worsted, wing tip shoes, a starched shirt,
a watch chain across his vest, brown fedora.

An unusual sight, then, thus attired,
walking the golf course as the doctor ordered.
Graciousness and self-deprecating humor
make him welcome to the foursomes he joins.

In a land where cotton is king
he was for decades a cotton broker.
The town playground bears his name.
He says he and Claire made it possible.

A woman friend of my mother's told me
Mr. Jim made and lost several fortunes.
I try to understand what that means.
He does not act as a rich man might.

I try to think about his life, his work.
I read he once had bank credit to cover 300 bales.
I imagine him giving the farmers a fair price.
Harder to imagine a younger Miss Claire.

∽

Married to Miss Claire over fifty years.
She can be a challenge like the Scots Irish she is.
They dote like attentive sweethearts,
he even more so near the end, in her senility.

Once I saw her growing frustrated, fidgety.
She turns angrily on him, accusing him
of far-fetched things, blame flung wildly about.
I had been prepared that this was happening.

He absorbs it stoically but looks deflated.
What can he be thinking as she fumes?
Surely he knows it's not the real she but
some lost fury breaking through tangled circuits

She was a few years older than Mr. Jim,
and he lived a few years after she died.
I went off to college, having learned from him.
He was curious about my progress to the end.

∽

A Remembrance of Mr. Jim says he was
"a man of deep integrity … always truthful and honest."
Earlier, I had seen that with my own eyes.
Mercy, the young me wondered, *can I be that man?*

First Friend

My best friend growing up died yesterday.
He'd just emailed me, now gone in the wind.
When he will seem dead, I cannot say.
He is still here, as real today as then.

Son of my minister, a preacher's boy,
suitor of my sister, a summer spree.
She was his youthful infatuation's joy.
For losing her, he blamed himself, not me.

He was thoughtful, reserved, truly brilliant.
His off-beat humor was a swift curve ball.
Much about him just a little different.
I loved the guy, the quirkiness and all.

I was the student body president
but he was the president of our class,
his four years as prez without precedent,
respected in ways I could not surpass.

He was a teacher, a Chaucer scholar,
a writer and a poet, prone to deep dives,
one who cared not a whit for the dollar,
father of four who didn't well fit his wives.

There may be a memorial service.
I am asking myself, why should I go.
It makes good sense to outwait the virus.
The family will not care if I show.

It won't be a gathering of old friends,
unlikely more than a simple good-bye,
some of them likely there to make amends,
then the proverbial blink of the eye.

Yet I am sure beyond doubt I'll attend.
I'll go if I am the only one there,
I want to say good-bye to my first friend,
respect his goodness, say my off-beat prayer.

The Six Seasons of New England

Greening

Beginning of everything,
the eternal return.
Explosions of chartreuse
a dozen shades,
viridescence
but ephemeral.
Crocuses poke up,
daffodils show their faces,
nature waking up.
Sap made it to your waffles.
A season of reassurance.

Garden

Means work, so much to do.
Days long and warm,
growing season short.
Everyone busy—
bringing in the hay,
setting out the garden,
putting up the dilly beans,
hoping for the rains.
Bluebirds reclaim their houses.
Baseball and no school.
A season of sustenance.

Foliage

is a harlequin duck,
impossible not to watch.
Colors joyous, playful.
Nature's grace,
free, bountiful, undeserved.
Ample old barns, orchards,
fat sheep, dwarf Nigerian goats,
county fairs with
draft horse pulls and pig races
blues and bluegrass.
A season of worship.

Stick

peaks in November.
Everything visible, exposed.
the land lies open.
It lacks color
but adds contour.
Stubble fields where
once grew hay and corn.
A thousand snow geese
feed in the Addison marshes.
There is a nip in the wind,
and snow on Camel's Hump.
A season of seeing.

Snow

seems forever.
Pumping the brakes won't
stop the slide into the ditch.
Before covid, cabin fever.
Yet for many snow makes
this place the joy that it is:
maple limbs dappled white,
snowmobile trails snake
through woods, crossing Nordic ones,
black diamond slopes awaiting.
Time for reading.
A season of contemplation.

Mud

is the dreaded one,
the curse on all
who use dirt roads,
and that is everyone.
Let's hear no more
of mud, glorious mud:
the mud is where cars sink to the axles.
Mud is a rite of passage,
mercifully short,
something that must be crossed
to find the Greening.
A season of anticipation.

Getting Close

A half-century ago my wife and I walked up
Jack Mountain into an unexplored meadow.
I held my little girl's hand in mine,
we carried our young sons on our backs.
It was summer, our sweatbands were
drenched, and we were exhausted. Still,

the scene ahead as we entered the meadow
startled us: everywhere white daisies
and Queen Anne's Lace, black-eyed Susans,
yellow yarrow, pink aster, purple thistle,
orange hawkweed and early goldenrod.
Our young daughter looked up at us and asked—

"Are we in Heaven?"

Just yesterday I was walking an old
logging road that runs uphill through
some green shade-dappled saplings
and opens out to a big meadow on top.
As I approached the meadow on the ridge,
all I could see ahead was the late day sun

sitting, pausing on the crest of the hill
and pouring a blinding gold over the horizon.
I just stood there in the saffron glow.
Two dark silhouettes were on the ridge top.
It took a second but then I recognized
my dogs standing there and waiting for me.

Someplace Safe

The dirt road to the farm in West Virginia
leaves the main road that runs beside
the South Branch of the Potomac
then heads up along a bare hill that
slopes off to the right into a mist-filled valley.
On the way there, station wagon filled,
three children restless, squabbling and teasing,
tired after the four hour drive from DC,
we pass by two old sheep farms on the left.
They mark the spot where we sing "almost heaven,"
and I think for a moment that I am John Denver.

After going there again last evening,
I awoke, startled—
this place is real only in my dreams.
I've been going there for decades
with my un-aging family in our 1970s car.
The dream never changes, and we never quite arrive.

We had an actual place on Jack Mountain in West Virginia,
a place my wife and kids loved with a view down the hollow
to the North Fork of the South Branch below.
The house had no plumbing, and the privy was a two-seater.
Mainly it was a weekend place for us but
once we stayed the summer fixing things, painting,
bringing back an old orchard and planting 500 tiny trees.
My hands developed calluses thicker than beech bark.
The place of my secret dream was not this place, but nearby.

So I dream,
opposing what was and is
with what could be, might be—
a place of happiness
apart from time and change and loss
somewhere and no where.

The Mistake: Merv's Story

There was an accident on the highway
early on Sunday morning, just yesterday,
not an interstate but a poor state road.
We had talked about it being a bad stretch.

I can hardly bring myself to tell this.
She was pregnant and so they're both gone now.
My house creaks and bangs from the cold and wind.
It was frozen hard like this yesterday.

My Sis was driving fast and hit black ice
on the curve near the Ace Hardware and slid
flat sideways into an oncoming truck.
He was carrying a load of white pine.

On Saturday night late she had over
a new guy she met in the bar in town,
a mistake way past a few too many.
He went about it in a rough mean way.

"I want the cute young one too," he said.
"That's my daughter," Sis yelled. "Forget it, jerk!"
But he forced Sally into the bathroom,
locked the door tight, and took his pleasure.

Come morning, Sis knew what she had to do.
With her dead husband's pistol beside her
on the old pickup seat, she headed out
to the place he was staying for the night.

When she hit the ice she was likely thinking
about where she should put the first bullet.
Perhaps she was thinking between his legs.
That is what I likely would be thinking.

Sally said my Sis held her tight all night,
told how she fought and got hit many times.
She cried, "I'm so sorry. I'm so sorry."
Her mom finally found the gun and left.

I have my gun but I have told the police.
For now, I'll give the cops a chance to act.
I'll take care of Sally as best I can.
But I have so little to offer her.

Sis should have gone to school but went to drugs.
She straightened out became a good mother.
She loved, protected and worked hard at it.
But she had a weak spot for drink and men.

I will miss her to the end of my days.
But Sally, my God, how can I help her?
How can we get beyond this awfulness
and claim a small place of peace in this world?

The Man in the Prius

Typical small village
in rural Vermont:
a town one road thick,
church of many denominations
among two dozen simple homes
holding hands along the road,
an elementary school on the hill,
and a town store
where I stop for milk.
Decent looking Prius
pulls up beside me
at the old gas pumps.
He goes inside to prepay.

Fifteen years here,
I've settled in.
So it took me a minute
to really see what
I had just taken for granted.

Man about 60, stocky, strong,
workman clothes, sawdust
on scuffed up boots,
a face behind a mask that said Vote.
Red Sox cap.

So, here was this Vermonter,
a working man, a long timer
not a retired import like me,
driving a fuel efficient vehicle
wearing a proper covid mask
beseeching the world to vote—
a scene simply taken in stride,
unremarkable here.

In the 2016 presidential election,
if only gun owners had voted,
Trump would have carried every state,
but one.

A Meal To Remember

Little place cards in pastel shades
each with a first name of a dear friend
at our dinner table over this past decade.
Quite a large collection now. I look
at them one by one, remembering it was when,
and whether there was a why or any reason—
these meals, before the isolating, sacramental.

I turn the cards face down, I shuffle them and
place four on the table. I turn them over again
and the party begins.
Ed is dead but he is here. He was our first friend in town.
Dear Cindy moved away to be near her children
but she is here too. Also Julian and Jim, a couple,
a graphic artist and a writer of funny novels.

I try to imagine what the group would like for dinner.
Vegetarian Cindy is easy.
It's Julian who can't eat onions who's hard.
Ottolenghi's maqluba is perfect I decide,
one version without chicken, another without onions.
I can smell the kitchen perfumed with baharat.

I remember the stories Jim told, his life-size rolling laugh.
The one about his failings at farming could be a novel itself.
And the time Ed said with a twinkle that
nothing in life had prepared him for his parents.
I heard Jim's laugh again just yesterday on zoom,
but it was no substitute for the real thing.

Like Snow

The snow's so slow,
it's barely falling.
The field is frozen solid,
the wind gone elsewhere.
Still, the fat fluffy flakes
dance and twirl and jump
trying to stay suspended.

It's time to take a walk
before the blizzard comes.
My legs are failing but
for now I am still able
to dance and twirl a bit.
I'll leave the jumping to Folly,
a dog who can suspend herself
like snow.

Stick Season 2020

Stick season is here!
The world is deciduous.
Fall foliage fallen.

Now I see their barn,
a red-green dot on the hill.
Far away, but not.

The way the land lies,
less color but more contour.
Just like our faces.

The last hay is in,
fields left to murders of crows.
Brown stubble looks gray.

Honkers overhead!
Chickadees flit and stay close.
We go south like geese.

Turkeys stride in lines.
Stick forest hides them quickly.
It hides great moose too.

Ash trees wait in fear.
Slender limbs reach to heaven,
offer anxious prayer.

Good friend passed away.
Buried before the ground froze.
No answer for loss.

Nature's shutting down.
She is going now to sleep.
White blanket needed.

Tall pine sentinels.
The evergreens do not sleep,
keep the woods secure.

Dusky dark at 4.
Soon the sun will be reborn.
Longer days ahead.

This year's almost done.
Anxiety was its name.
Tree limbs wave with joy!

Calm now in the woods.
A quiet settles in and spreads.
For the moment, peace.

Put out the brain fire!
Settle your mind in the heart.
Let your new eye see.

Dove Hunting

1.

Two hunters walking
into the cornfield
on a fine fall day,
an old farmer and me
when I was thirteen.
Do you want a chaw?
offering me tobacco.
The man I surely was
took a generous bite.
We walked our ways,
built our cornstalk blinds.
Only soon I realized
my mouth was full of juice,
my cheeks a chipmunk's.
What was I supposed to do?
Of course swallow the juice.
My world went dizzy,
I was nauseated,
and then, BLAM!
my gun went off.
As I sat there in the dirt,
earth and sky spinning,
shotgun several feet away,
I looked up at the farmer
standing over me,
staring with concern.
"Are you all right?" he asked.
I wanted to explain.
And he said, "You shot me.
But I'm okay. Stings a bit."

2.

Another time, the hunt over,
Dad and I walking out of the field
as dusk approached,
birds in our jackets or the trees.
Then one last dove enters the field
flying high, and someone yells,
"Mark!" Everyone drops to one knee.
When the bird is overhead
almost too far to shoot,
Dad says, "Take it, Gus."
I am flummoxed at first.
But I stand and fire my 20-gauge,
and the poor bird falls to our feet.
I was very proud that day.
And Dad was proud too.

I see it differently now.
The graceful mourning doves
enjoy the sunflower seeds
under our bird feeders
here on our Vermont hill.
They gather, rest on ledges,
make their cooing sounds,
not all mournful.
They sit on our windowsill
looking in at me with their big black eyes,
and I hope they are saying
they hold no grudges.

Song of the South

I thank my Momma
and my Daddy too.
Thanks to them,
I got this song for you.

Birthday is tomorrow.
I'm an old man now.
I tried so hard but
it doesn't matter anyhow.

I grew up with racists.
There's so much to blame.
It's what history did,
to our ever-lasting shame.

I see a person,
there's a battle I can't win.
A thing I still notice is
the color of their skin.

It is a curse I think,
a present from the South.
Some things I used to say
banished from my mouth.

Momma had a kind heart,
but Daddy had it bad.
The 1950's hit him hard.
At first it made him mad.

He began to teach
in a school for only whites.
Math for little white kids—
so much for civil rights.

There came a point
something happened to my Dad.
He liked so many Blacks the
teaching began to make him sad.

He joined the War on Poverty,
worked with Blacks every day.
He knew from his own life
they were people in every way.

Daddy was a smart man.
It couldn't be shut out:
his Black friends were equals,
not something he could doubt.

He didn't tell me what to think.
I could think for myself.
But he helped my life along
to become something else.

The curse I carry forward.
Soon I'll find my grave.
But I hope I have respected
the gift my Daddy gave.

An Error in Time and Space

You are gone tonight, and the vacant space
beside me is a vastness into which I reach.

I feel only absence and longing,
cold sheets in a wintry November.

There is a not rightness about it,
an error in time and space.

I remember two weeks ago dining
out across the river with easy friends.

While waiting for the food to arrive,
we went around the table answering—

what is the secret of a long marriage,
since we had all been long married.

Spurred by the moment, I answered
devotion, loyalty, forgiveness.

I should have remembered the words
stitched on the pillow in your chair:

Happiness is being married to your best friend.
I long for my friend this night.

Lift Up These Eyes

We chased away the mist,
opened up the day,
blew holes in the clouds,
and called down the sun.
It lit the wet rocks where
we dropped to our knees,
leaned over the edge, followed
the red talus slope down and down
as it fell to green embroidery
framing the dark river below.

The breeze began to stir.
We heard the tent door flap.
Little Cas is crawling out
into the morning light. She lifts
her head, sees us, and sends
an ear-to-ear crescent-eyed grin—
a moment of shared delight
as bright as the new found sun.
Good morning, Cas, we say
in all the languages we know.

3

Save Time to Smile

)

The Devil's Assistant's Dictionary

Ambrose Bierce was a very clever guy
with the mind of a troublesome fairy.
For years he scribbled little notes
that became *The Devil's Dictionary*.

His definitions always cut somewhere.
Once he set out to define harangue.
He said it was "a speech by an opponent,
who is known as an harangue-outang."

Most often his quips were more adult,
but I am setting the bar low for myself.
I too have been at work on a dictionary.
I may one day join Bierce, as his elf.

Our language has many big gaps,
holes that need lexical cementing.
So I am creating some brave new words.
I'll start now with their inventing.

Pandammit – a situation of everything going awry
with no good options, as in "His life in a pandammit,
he lived in his sweatpants."

Exasperational – a condition of having high
goals you know are hopeless, as in "She lived an
exasperational life, with her soufflés always collapsing."

Slah – an adult child. Said to be derived from "still living at home."

Complinots – praise or compliments that are known by giver to be undeserved, as in "She layered on the complinots so that he would continue the cooking, sketchy as it was."

Complifish – compliments given in hopes of compliments in return, as in "He complifished his neighbor about her garden but got nothing but a 'thank you' in return."

Ambadassador – someone commissioned to spread disruption, as in "They sent an ambadassador to the anti-vax rally."

Mellowdrama – life when high, as in "In another mellowdramatic incident, the police stopped him as he was walking down the center line half naked."

Disastrophy – a really bad, cataclysmic event, as in "Given climate change, Prometheus stealing fire from the gods was, longterm, a disastrophy."

Awsomistic – to have a dream or vision that is awe-inspiring and that one believes is going to be realized, as in "Awsomistically, his fans believe that Tom Brady will win Super Bowls forever."

Flushtrate – repeated failure to get the toilet to work, as in, "I'm totally flushtrated with that damn thing!"

Fontrum – embarrassment for someone who isn't embarrassed but clearly should be, as in "Hear that silence from his audience? Lots of fontrum in here."

Enterfailedment – a box office bomb, a TV series canceled mid-season, the comic who dies onstage, as in "The commercial gods declared the Shakespeare film enterfailment."*

*For a few, I offer thanks.

Radiculus

"Radiculopathy"
is the perfect name for it!
Pinched nerves commandeer muscles
making them mere receptacles
for a big pain in the buttacle.

"Laminectomy"
is quite apt also!
If it sounds just like
the neck is coming off,
well, that's quite close to
the truth of the matter.
The pain is 'cruciating.
I must be mad as a hatter.

I long for simple days of
appendectomy
and tonsillectomy!
That was at the beginning of life,
not now near the end of me.
And if they offer again the knife?
Maybe I will just wait and see.

I may not have to wait too long.
I can clear hear old Charon's song.
I'm sure the emperor of malady
is waiting there for aging me.
Problems now lurk around my door.
I thought I had a long time more!

Thanks to Weezie

My son's dog once got in stickers;
he quickly lay down in a heap.
Weezie went there to comfort him,
and she pulled them out with her teeth.

When Weezie was young and alone
and she could not hold it any more,
she went upstairs to the bathroom—
did her puddle on the hard tile floor.

Weezie slid down a big ice hill.
She got caught in a bramble pile.
I went down the hill to free her,
and she gave me a big dog smile.

She would always ask permission,
and had a most beautiful way.
School kids loved to take her to play.
At the end I tried to say, "Stay."

Scientists do major testing
to see if dogs have human feelings.
Lordy, one then must ask aloud:
What's it that needs more revealing?

I'll leave you with a conviction,
one I first found in my old heart.
These dogs, there is nothing better
in which we humans had a part.

Golden Okra

Ocracoke is lovely the way
little beach villages once were
and still should be today—
an island worth remembering,
a restful, pleasant place to stay.

It was on lovely Ocracoke
in our cute little space
when she said, "it's stuffy,"
and set my mind to race.
She likes piles of covers and
banishes breezes to the beach,
so I worry what she meant
in her short two-word speech.
Can it be the company's stuffy,
when it's just me here with her?
I know that I can be fussy,
but am I also getting stuffy?

Home now from Ocracoke,
I hang golden okra in the window,
sold there as Christmas ornaments,
hung here with adoration and thanks.
I dutifully recall my first taste of okra:
too slimy to be high in any ranks.
But okra worship begins in earnest
with first frying in the old oil tank,
golden crisp and simply heavenly.
I don't listen now to okra cranks.

I stare at the golden okra
and still wonder what she meant.
I know that I am changing,
but in directions to lament?
I'm flinging the windows open,
letting the breeze blow through.
I'll continue just as I am, and
see if this room's stuffy too!

Callie, the Prodigal Dog

The prodigal dog is the one full of DEET,
not the calm one sitting here at my feet.
I wish there were something I could do.
Instead I'll just wait here, and I'll stew.

Wherever there's DEET she will lick it.
It's a habit now; she can't kick it.
It's only one of her profligate ways.
Mostly she just teases and plays.

Her big sister listens so well.
She's slower but does what you tell.
The prodigal dog is much brighter,
but there's nothing on earth I can teach her.

Problem is, she's cute as can be.
She does tricks you definitely should see.
She amuses her parents so greatly.
Have you seen what she's done just lately?

So we shower her with oohs and aahs,
while big sis sits watching for cars.
Sometimes big sis gets quite jealous,
which she clearly knows how to tell us.

Time and talent are going to waste
as Callie grows up at her playful pace.
She's not a puppy any more.
Did you see her levitate off the floor?

With apologies to my friend Folly, the best,
a finer dog than this poem suggests.
She's the de facto mom of our little pest.
With her, we are just doubly blessed.

What Callie knows was taught by Folly.
Lab things, not those of the border collie.
Big sis Folly is patient endlessly
as Callie tugs her jowls relentlessly.

This verse must have a happy ending.
But life with Callie is just beginning.
Do I hope that she'll get serious?
Giving bugs leeway for biting us?
I am sure Callie will grow up fine.
It's all just a matter of time.

God's Own Black Flies

God walked into the garden.
He saw that it was good.
Mostly.

He noticed that horned tomato worms
were decimating the plants and
beetles were ruining his potatoes.

Leaning down, He asked them loudly,
"Who the hell made you?"

And in that moment they found Him.
A natural poet, He cried out:

"Black flies, black flies, you're here again!
You found my forehead and my chin.
Black flies, black flies, oh, what a pest.
It's time you guys *also* took a rest."

And then the devil tempted Him—

"Black flies, I want you to go for hair
that's orange in the atmosphere.
Not a little girl's, for sure,
but a man far more immature!"

His good nature soon returning,
God remembered his Creation.
He paused, thought, and said wistfully,

"Black flies, if only I could clearly see
you as part of biodiversity!"

World Changing, Northern Perspective

Black flies now have competition
in creating a foretaste of perdition.
I refer of course to the disgusting tick,
the bug that made a good friend sick.
They've now spread northward day by day
as global warming has paved the way.
Before their presence becomes a flood
and they abscond with all our blood,
we must act with strong convictions
to prevent even worse afflictions.
Climate change is messing with the season,
ringing ever more degrees in.
It's not just ticks it's bringing you.
Soon it will also bring kudzu.
With kudzu comes the mite-y diggers:
the tender curse of summer chiggers.
The human body is just delightful
to all the bugs that get a bite full.
Nor are our poor bodies immune
from the torrid heat waves coming soon.
Even rattlesnakes may be in store,
if you want to worry even more.
But please don't blame me for warning.
It's time for truth about global warming.

Climate Negotiations

Brazil's new plans for Amazon destruction
are what prompted its abrupt decision
not to host world climate negotiations.

Now the small island nation of José Cuervo
has become an international hero
for bravely stepping into the breach.

Its main proffers are, first, its beach
with cabanas to watch the erosion.
Then, diving on reefs newly bleached,

the few fish now caught by explosions.
But most important for negotiators *arriva*:
unlimited quantities of blue agave tequila!

Hey, You Males!

Hey, you males,
do you ever feel like
a praying mantis,
the weaker sex
here for procreation
then dispensable,
even devourable,
by the new woman?
She is tough, resilient,
smart, and she persists.
Some reward, I say,
for the great state of
the world we made
in countless generations
of our manly leadership!
I think about rising up, or
maybe just speaking out,
but I am too tired
and my back hurts, and
privately, I think women
are right about us.

When We Were Just Four

We were just four,
playing on the floor
of Billy's big side porch,
when along came a spider
and sat close beside us.

There is a lot still to go
if you're a boy of four,
so much you need to know.
We found a toy by the door,
gave that poor spider a blow.

When what should appear
from under that toy but
a hundred tiny spiders
spreading out around us,
many headed straight
for our little bare legs,
tiny spiders coming
faster and faster.

Needless to say
we hurried away
ran quick from that place,
and hid somewhere safe—
in Billy's mom's skirt
in the kitchen.

On that summer day
in a time far away,
I learned a lesson for sure.
It's now a cliché but
its warning rings true:
'Tis best not to mess
with Mother Nature.

A Morning Around New Year's Day

Real Vermonters love
a morning like this,
a land of ice and snow,
clear, crisp, and 5 below.
The purple shadows
from big bare maples
reach out across
the slopes and rolls.
The big balsam bows
with her new white coat
while the birdhouses
wear their snowcaps
and the swings try out
their new white loads as
the wind gives easy pushes.
Once-green everything
now everywhere white
except the red of sumac.
The deer will browse at dusk
but now what moves are
chickadees flitting and flying
with their friends the juncos.
There are a few goldfinch
at the feeders, but they left
their gold somewhere safe.

The dogs bark when the
long-hanging roof ice
drops in a noisy plump.
It is a beautiful day
for a walk on the road
or to head out with
skis or snowshoes,
and also very nice to return
to a warm sweet-smelling house.

Still, my wife and I were raised in warmer climes.
In a month or so we will be chilled enough to
take out of the refrigerator and be enjoyed
by friends and family on the beach in Carolina.

Author's Note

There are mostly new poems here, but I have
augmented them with some from my earlier books,
especially where they seemed a natural fit. There's
also a new pantoum, a villanelle, and two poems in
haiku. Who would have thought?

I am quite indebted to many for their help.
A special appreciation is due to Baron Wormser,
Jonathan Stableford, Anne Pace, Syd Lea,
Debbi Wraga, Mary Evelyn Tucker, John Grim,
Ina Anderson, Richard Garcia, Catherine
McCullough, Byron Breese, Carol Potter, and
Cece Speth. My thanks to all for your patience,
good advice, and support.

I hope you enjoy these efforts.

Gus Speth
Strafford Vermont
Summer 2021

CPSIA information can be obtained
at www.ICGtesting.com
Printed in the USA
BVHW032056181121
621664BV00008B/6